Windows 10

A Complete Guide to Using

Windows 10

Table of Contents

Introduction

Windows 10 is the latest operating system offered by Microsoft. It was designed and developed for personal computers, embedded devices, tablets, and other Internet of Things (IoT) devices.

Windows 10 was launched in July 2015 as a successor to Windows 8. Ever since the release of Windows 10, Microsoft has continuously made clarifications about how they will keep upgrading Windows 10 perpetually over introducing a new Windows operating system altogether.

Anyone with a Windows 7 or Windows 8 operating system on their machine can upgrade seamlessly to Windows 10 without having to format their existing file system or deleting existing data. The upgrade is as simple as running the Windows 10 installer that transfers all settings and data from the existing Windows 7 or Windows 8 system onto the new Windows 10 system. The installer also gives you the option to customize your upgrade by selecting what you want to keep and what you want to erase during the installation. Users can wait for an automatic upgrade prompt in their current Windows 7 or Windows 8 operating systems, or they can manually download the Windows Update Assistant from Microsoft's website to upgrade their Windows system proactively.

There is also a variant of Windows 10 known as Windows 10 Mobile that is an operating system developed by Microsoft for smartphones.

We will learn about all that and more throughout the following chapters. Thank you for choosing this book, I hope you find it to be helpful.

Chapter One: About Windows 10

Windows 10 brings back the tiled start menu that was introduced in Windows 8 and was a major upgrade from the Windows 7 start menu. For tablet users or personal computers with touch screens, users can experience the touch-focused start menu as well, which can be activated separately. Users can alternate between a touchscreen and keyboard on devices that support the switch using Microsoft Continuum. Continuum automatically detects the type of device in use and switches the interface to match the device.

Windows 10 offers an integrated search that can be used to search the local locations of the system as well as the Internet parallely.

Internet Explorer has been replaced by Microsoft Edge in Windows 10, which takes over the role of the primary web browser. Edge has evolved as a chromium-based browser in 2020 to work at par with web browsers such as Google Chrome and Mozilla Firefox. Edge offers integrated tools such as Web Notes and Reading Views. Users can use Web Notes to mark up their favorite websites, whereas Reading Views allows users to view most websites without the ads on them. The Edge browser has inbuilt integration with Cortana, the digital assistant by Microsoft.

Cortana's search is integrated with Microsoft's Bing search engine, and allows search in the form of both text and voice. Cortana saves user preferences such as their location, browsing history, search history, applications, and services used within the system, to offer a customized operating system experience to the user. Cortana can be disabled at any point in time if not needed.

Security in Windows 10

Windows 10 offers integrated multi-factor authentication support through technologies such as smartcards and tokens. With Windows Hello, Microsoft also introduced biometric authentication for users through fingerprint scan, facial recognition, and iris scan.

The Windows 10 operating system also offers virtualization-based tools for security such as Windows Defender Device Guard, Isolated User Mode, and Windows Defender Credential Guard. These security features safeguard data, user credentials, and processes, so that the risk of damage from any attack can be minimized.

The BitLocker encryption tool has also evolved with Windows 10, and it safeguards any data that is in motion between devices via email, storage hardware, and cloud services.

Hardware Requirements for Windows 10

You need the following system requirements as a minimum to install Windows 10 on your computer:

- **Processor:** 1GHz or faster

- **RAM:** 1 GB for a 32-bit installation and 2 GB for a 64-bit installation

- **Hard Disk Space:** 16 GB for a 32-bit installation and 20 GB for a 64-bit installation

- **Graphics Card:** DirectX 9 or above support with Windows Display Driver Model 1.0

- **Display:** At least a resolution of 800x600 pixels

Installing Windows 10 on a smartphone requires a minimum of 1 GB RAM, 8 GB of disk space, 32 Bit color per pixel, and at least a 720p resolution. Smartphones also need to have a SnapDragon processor by Qualcomm.

Upgrades to Windows 10

There are two options available to upgrade your system to Windows 10 from Windows 7 or Windows 8.1. The first way is to install and run the "Get Windows 10 application" that can be downloaded from Microsoft's website. Another way is to download the image file for Windows 10 from Microsoft's website, load it onto a bootable media, and run the installation.

If you have been a Windows XP user over the past years, unfortunately, a Windows 10 install will have to be a clean install, and none of your settings or files will be migrated automatically to the Windows 10 system. This is because there are compatibility issues between Windows XP and Windows 10, since Windows XP is a very old operating system.

Updates in Windows 10

Windows 10 has four licensing structures known as branches that control the medium and time for Windows 10 updates on various devices.

There is a Microsoft Insiders Program that gives updates to members of the program as a preview to the changes in the operating system. This branch makes the update available to the members before it is made available to general users. Therefore, they get time to test out the new features and report bugs, if any.

The next branch is known as the Current Branch, which pushes updates automatically to consumers with a Windows 10 device. It is however necessary that the device has Internet connectivity and that automatic updates are enabled.

The Current Branch for Business is a branch that focuses on enterprise clients. It is available for a select few versions of Windows 10 such as Professional, Education, and Enterprise. It allows an IT team to preview the update for 4 months, and then they have another 8 months to apply the update. If the IT team fails to apply the update within the 8 months, they can risk losing support from Microsoft.

The last branch of Windows 10 updates is known as the Long-Term Servicing Branch or LTSB in short. This update branch is designed for Windows devices that cannot afford any downtime for updates that are pushed in short intervals. These devices comprise emergency room devices, ATMs, and the like, where updates are pushed at an interval of two to three years. The updates to such systems can also be delayed up to a maximum of 10 years. If the update is not applied beyond 10 years, support from Microsoft can be lost.

Irrespective of the branch of update preferred by an organization, the updates ensure that their Windows 10 systems are patched for vulnerabilities and that the operating system runs smoothly.

History of Windows 10

Microsoft provided a major upgrade to its Windows line of operating systems when they introduced Windows 8. Windows

8 brought a fresh new interface with support for touch-based devices such as smartphones and tablets. However, it did not provide the same level of convenience and user-friendliness to traditional devices such as desktops and laptops. Microsoft launched Windows 10 to address these shortcomings of the Windows 8 operating system.

Windows 10 was announced in September 2014, and Microsoft immediately provided a preview of Windows 10 the very next month to members of the Microsoft Insiders Program. They later launched Windows 10 for general consumers in July 2015. The vast majority of consumers received Windows 10 with a smile on their face as they accepted that it was user-friendlier compared to Windows 8 due to its traditional layout and similarities to Windows 7. The Windows 10 operating system also garnered a lot of support due to improved performance over past versions of Windows and its search efficiency via Cortana integration.

Microsoft launched the Windows 10 Anniversary update in August 2016, which brought positive changes to the Start Menu and Taskbar. Browser extensions to Microsoft Edge were also released with this update.

The April 2017 update for Windows 10 brought in the Creators Update that improved the Windows Hello facial recognition technology. It also allowed users to save Microsoft Edge tabs to view them later.

Another update was launched in October 2017, which introduced Windows Defender Zero Guard to the system for protection against zero-day attacks. It also made provisions for system admins or IT staff to put background applications into an energy-efficient mode, to improve battery life and performance.

The August 2019 update introduced various new keyboard layouts to help improve the experience for Windows 10 tablet users.

Privacy in Windows 10

Microsoft collects a lot of data from its users concerning settings, crashes, usernames, passwords, contact lists, and IP addresses, among other things. However, you do have an option to set a limit on the amount of data collected by Microsoft. There are three levels of settings to set a limit on the data sent by your Windows 10 system to Microsoft:

- Basic

- Full

- Enhanced

By default, this is set to Enhanced, and almost all data is sent to Microsoft. This can be changed easily to the other two options. Users of Windows 10 Enterprise or Education have an option to disable data collection by Microsoft altogether.

Microsoft does not read user data at personal levels, as it is anonymized. The privacy statement released by Microsoft states that it collects data to improve the operating system and work towards creating a better user experience.

Chapter Two: Using Windows 10

If you have recently purchased a new Windows 10 machine or have upgraded your existing machine to Windows 10, this chapter will take you through the basics of using your new Windows 10 operating system. Note that this chapter refers to using Windows 10 on a desktop, and if you are using a Windows 10 laptop, some sections may differ slightly for you.

Let us go through the various sections of using your new Windows 10 system one by one.

Getting Started

Logging into Windows 10

When you switch on your Windows 10 system for the very first time, you will be prompted to create a Microsoft account if you don't already have one. After this, you will always be required to login to the system using your Microsoft account username and password. You can also skip this and create a local user on the system, but it is advisable to create a Microsoft Account so that your settings are synced across multiple Microsoft devices you may own.

Desktop Navigation

After you have logged in using your Microsoft account, you will be presented with the Microsoft Desktop. The desktop is the primary workspace of your Windows 10 system. It allows you to view and manage your applications, and files. You can also access the Internet from the web browsers available in your desktop space.

Launching Applications

The most important thing on your desktop is the Windows 10 Start Menu. You can use the start menu to open various applications that are installed on your system, just like you did in the previous versions of Windows. Click on the start menu in the bottom left corner of your desktop screen and then click on the required application. If you do not see the application you want to open, you can simply click on *All Applications* to get a full list of applications on your system.

Accessing Files

You can access files and folders in Windows 10 using the File Explorer. You can launch the file explorer by clicking on its icon on the taskbar. Alternatively, you can also click on any folder on your desktop to launch the file explorer.

Searching for Files or Applications

You can search for a specific file or application on your Windows 10 system by clicking on the Start Button and then by simply typing out the keyword for your search. Alternatively, the Windows key on your keyboard will also open up the search utility.

Adjusting your Settings

The most important settings for your Windows 10 system can be changed using the Settings app. It lets you change things like your display settings, network settings, and more. You can access the Settings app by clicking on the start menu and selecting settings. Like the past versions of Windows, you can also make changes to your settings from the Control Panel. However, there are certain options such as adding a new user that are only available in the Settings app. Therefore, you will use the Settings app more often in Windows 10.

Shutting down Windows 10

After you are done with all your tasks on your Windows 10 system, ensure that you shut it down the right way. You can do this by clicking on the start menu, then selecting Power > Shut Down.

Managing Multiple Windows

An operating system is deemed to be most efficient if it lets you multitask. There are several tools and features in Windows 10 that serve this requirement. Let us go through these features one by one.

Snap

The snap feature in Windows 10 helps you resize various windows. This is a good feature when you need two windows adjacent to each other. You can do this by dragging one window to the right or left edge of the desktop screen. Release the mouse after this. The window will snap onto that half of the screen. You can simply drag the window anywhere to unsnap it again.

If you have multiple windows, you can snap the other window to the empty side.

Flip

Flip is a simple feature that helps you to toggle between multiple open windows. You can do this by holding the ALT and TAB keys on your keyboard simultaneously, and then pressing the tab key until you reach the desired window.

Task View

The Task view feature is much like Flip, with a few differences. You can use the task view by clicking on the task view icon on the taskbar on the left. You can alternatively use the keyboard shortcut Windows key + Tab to launch the task view. This feature will present all open windows to you, and from there you can simply select the window you wish to go to.

Virtual Desktops

It can get very hectic to maintain multiple windows open on one single desktop. Windows 10 offers virtual desktops, allowing you to move some windows to the virtual desktop to avoid cluttering. The previous versions of Windows did not have this feature, but it has proved to be very useful since its introduction in Windows 10. You can create a new desktop by launching the task view and then clicking on New Desktop in the top-left corner.

After creating multiple virtual desktops, you can switch between them by using the task view. You can also move windows from one virtual desktop to another. To do this, simply open the task view, and drag a window from one desktop to the desired desktop.

You can close a virtual desktop by clicking on the X symbol in the top-right corner of the virtual desktop you wish to close.

Showing the Desktop

There will be times when you have multiple windows open at the same time and wish to go back to the desktop. Minimizing each window individually is a lot of effort for this. Fortunately, in Windows 10 there is an easy way to minimize all windows at once. You can do this by clicking on the bottom-right corner of your desktop. This will instantly minimize all open windows and reveal the desktop to you. If you want to restore all open windows, you just need to click on it again.

Personalizing your Windows 10 Desktop

You can make customizations to the looks of your Windows 10 desktop very easily. You can access the personalization settings by simply right clicking on the desktop screen and then selecting Personalization from the dropdown. This will present the personalization settings to you.

The personalization screen will present the following options to you:

- You can change the background of your desktop. This is the wallpaper feature that was there in the previous versions of Windows.

- You can also change the color scheme of your system.

- You can customize your lock screen. This includes the background that appears on your lock screen and the widgets such as temperature, time, etc.

- The themes option lets you customize your Windows 10 system to a predefined theme concerning the background wallpaper, the colors, the lock screen, etc.

- You can use the font option to change the font type and font size for your Windows system.

- The options for Start and Taskbar will let you personalize your start menu and taskbar.

Customizing the Start Menu

The start menu is one of the most popular features of Windows 10. The start menu is used to do multiple things such as launching apps, accessing recent folders, and more. You may feel the need to customize the start menu, since you will be accessing it regularly when using the Windows 10 system.

History of Start Menu

Up to Windows 7, the start menu was a narrow column. When Windows 8 was launched, the start menu was expanded to a start screen that was large, comprising a full-screen menu.

The new start menu faced a lot of criticism as users found it unnecessarily confusing. Therefore, the older start menu was added back with the release of Windows 10. The start menu in Windows 10 is similar to the Start menu in older versions of Windows before Windows 8. In addition to that, it also incorporates tiles that were introduced in Windows 8.

Rearranging Tiles

Windows 10 gives you the option to rearrange tiles as per your needs. You can select a tile and drag it to a different location. You can right-click on a tile to change its size as well.

Pinning/Unpinning Tiles

If there is a tile that is not present on the start menu by default and you want to add it, you can use the Pin option to pin it to the start menu. On the start menu, select the application of your choice, right-click on it, and select Pin to start.

This will pin the app to the start menu.

Similarly, you can right-click on a pinned app on the start menu, and click on Unpin from Start, to unpin it.

Turning Off Live Tiles

You may notice that a few tiles on the start menu in Windows 10 such as the calendar, mail, and weather, are animated. These are known as live tiles. These have an advantage in that they show live data to you. For example, if a new email has arrived and you haven't read it, it will keep showing up on the tile. However, this can be distracting for some users and they may want to turn the live tile off. This can be done by right clicking on the desired tile and selecting Turn live tile off.

Other Options for Start Menu

There are a few other customizations that you can make to the start menu, such as viewing the start menu in full screen. You can access these options by right clicking on the desktop and clicking on Personalize from the dropdown. Then select Start on the tool that pops up. You can choose to enable or disable the following start menu features:

- Show most used apps

- Show recently added apps

- Use Start full screen

- Show recently opened items in Jump Lists on Start or the taskbar

Making Windows 10 Look Familiar

When Microsoft launched Windows 8 in 2012, the biggest feedback all users provided was that it was difficult to use. In response to this, Microsoft brought back some design features from older versions of Windows for the launch of Windows 10. Windows 10 may still have some things that might confuse you or annoy you, but there are certain customizations you can make to Windows 10 that will give it the nostalgic feel of Windows 7, or Windows XP.

Simplifying the Start Menu

When you click on the Start button of Windows 10, you will see that it uses an expanded start menu that is larger compared to the start menus from the previous versions of Windows. However, if you want to have the same old traditional and narrow start menu from the previous versions of Windows, the very first thing to do is to unpin all the tiles that appear on your Windows 10 start menu. You can do so by right clicking on the tiles that appear on the start menu and selecting Unpin from Start in the dropdown.

After you have unpinned all the tiles from the Start Menu, you can just take your mouse pointer to the right edge and drag the start menu towards the left to make it narrow.

Hiding Cortana

One of the highlights of Windows 10 is Cortana. It is a virtual search assistant that can help you find files or apps on the local system, or the Internet, simultaneously. However, there are users who prefer to not use a virtual assistant for search, and instead, do their searches manually. You can hide the Cortana icon by right clicking on the taskbar and selecting Cortana > Hidden.

Using Control Panel Instead of the Settings App

The Settings app on Windows 10 is used to make most of the changes to your system, unlike the Control Panel, which was how the Windows system was changed in the previous versions. However, the Control Panel still has a lot of options to make changes, and it has redirects to the Settings App whenever needed. You can launch the control panel by hitting the Windows key on your keyboard and typing Control Panel, followed by a hit on the Enter key.

User Management and Parental Controls

As we have already discussed, you need a user account to login to your Windows 10 system. Your system will have one account by default, the one that you set up while installing Windows 10.

However, if you have other people who will share the same Windows 10 system, you can create separate user accounts for every individual that will be using the computer.

We already know that creating a new user through a Microsoft account is the best way to get all the features of Windows. However, if a Microsoft account is not preferred, you can also create a local user that exists only on this system.

Note that you need to be the admin user on the Windows 10 system to create additional users.

Adding a New User (Microsoft Account)

You can follow the steps below to add a new user with a Microsoft Account.

1. Launch the Settings app and click on Accounts.

2. Select Family & Other Users. Navigate to the Other Users section and then click on Add someone else to this PC.

3. Enter the Microsoft username (email ID) of the user that you wish to add and click on Next.

4. The user will get added and can now login to the Windows 10 system using their Microsoft username. Note that the first login for the user may take several minutes.

Adding a New User (Local Account)

You can follow the steps below to add a new user without a Microsoft Account.

1. Launch the Settings app and click on Accounts.

2. Select Family & Other Users. Navigate to the Other Users section and then click on Add someone else to this PC.

3. Select the option that says, "The person I want to add does not have an email address".

4. You will be presented with an account creation screen. Select the option that says, "Add a user without a Microsoft account".

5. Input a username, and then create a password for the user. Make sure that you use a strong password. Click on Next.

6. The local user will now be able to login to the Windows 10 system.

Signing Out or Switching a User

When you are done using the system, you could shut the system down or simply sign out. To sign out, you can click on the Start button, select the user symbol on the left side, and you will be given the option to Sign Out. This will take the system to the lock screen, from where other users can log in.

A user doesn't need to sign out for another user to sign in. You can simply lock your account by following the same steps as above and clicking on Lock instead of Sign Out. This will simply lock your account, keep your session and apps intact, and take the system to the lock screen, from where another user can still log in and use the system. When the other user is done using the system and locks or signs out, you can log in again and you will be at the same point where you left your system when you locked it.

Managing User Accounts

The account created by you while installing Windows 10 is an administrator account by default. An administrator account is a superuser account that has all the rights and privileges to the system. The admin account can add new users and assign roles to those users as well. When you create a new user, it becomes a standard user account by default, which has normal rights and privileges to the system needed by most regular users. On a shared computer, one administrator account is sufficient, but you can make another user and administrator too if needed.

You can follow the steps below to convert a standard user account to an administrator user account.

1. Open the Setting app.

2. Go to Accounts.

3. Select the required user from the Family & other users option and click on Change account type.

4. From the dropdown provided, select Administrator, and then click on OK.

5. The selected user will now have administrator-level privileges on the system.

Setting up Parental Controls

Windows 10 offers parental controls to monitor your children's activities and safeguard them against inappropriate content. There is an option wherein you can:

- Restrict specific apps and websites.

- Set a time that your children can log in to the system.

This can be done by creating a family account for every child. The user must have a Microsoft account, as parental controls cannot be set for a local account.

You can do this by following the steps below.

1. Launch the Settings app.

2. Go to Accounts.

3. Click on Family & other users and select Add a family member.

4. Select Add a child, input their email address, and then click on Next.

5. You will need to verify the account by clicking on a link in the email that is sent to their email address.

6. After verifying the email address, click on Manage family settings online.

7. A website will open where you can select various options to set up parental controls.

You can view and control the following things from parental control:

- Recent activity

- Web browsing

- Apps & games

- Screen time

Security in Windows 10

There are numerous inbuilt features in Windows 10 to protect your computer against malware, viruses, and more. Let us go through the security feature list in Windows 10 to see how you can use it best.

User Account Control

This feature notifies you when another user or a program tries to change the system settings. When this happens, the screen gets locked temporarily and will require an administrator to approve changes. This helps to safeguard your system against accidental changes and malware. The feature also lets you decide the frequency at which you will see these warnings.

Windows Defender

Windows defender is an inbuilt antivirus security system to protect your computer against viruses and malware. You can use windows defender to scan your system manually when required. At the same time, it also provides real-time protection by scanning every file and app you access in real-time without slowing down the system.

Windows Firewall

Windows 10 has an inbuilt firewall that protects your system's connection to the Internet. A firewall will safeguard your system against unauthorized connections from outside. It also protects your system against network threats that can damage your system.

Windows Smart Screen

There is a full-screen warning that comes up, known as the smart screen warning, whenever a threat is detected from a file or application. Whenever you see this screen, it is advisable to not open the file or application unless you are sure that the file or application is legitimate.

Updating Windows

Microsoft provides regular and automatic updates to your Windows system. These updates include security patches, and new features, too. You can also manually check for updates and schedule an installation time for them. You can follow the steps below for viewing Windows Updates.

1. Launch the Settings app.

2. Select Updates & security.

3. You can now check if updates are available, or even set preferences for updates.

There are times when a new feature that is rolled out with an update has bugs. If you are aware of a particular update having bugs, you can defer that update, too. This does not mean that you can avoid the update altogether, but you will at least not receive the update immediately upon its release. This means that if a particular update has bugs; your system will still be at lower risk since you deferred the update.

You can follow these steps to defer updates.

1. Go to the Update and Security settings in the Settings app and click on advanced options.

2. Check the box that says Defer updates.

3. Your updates for Windows 10 will now be deferred. Note that important security updates will continue to get pushed to your system automatically from Microsoft.

Backup and Recovery

Windows 10 has an option wherein you can create a backup on an external hard drive to protect your files in the event of accidental data loss. This means that you can be at peace knowing your files are safe, even if something goes wrong with your Windows system.

You can do this by going to Updates & Security in the Settings app, and then selecting Backup from there. You can then select an external hard drive from here to start the backup process.

Similarly, once you have a backup ready, you can use the Recovery option to restore the lost files or reset your windows system to the default settings.

Why should you upgrade to Windows 10?

Windows 10 is the latest operating system by Microsoft for personal and enterprise devices. Most users accepted Windows 10 positively, but it did receive some criticism in 2016 since Microsoft was forcing users of the older versions to upgrade to Windows 10. There were complaints that many users were not given the option to skip the upgrade, and in many cases, their systems were upgraded without their consent or knowledge. Despite this, we would still suggest that upgrading your system to Windows 10 is a good thing.

Note: Windows 10 free upgrade ended in July 2016, and you will need to pay for a copy of Windows 10 now. You can purchase it from Microsoft's website.

There is a possibility that you are happy and content with your current version of Windows and are wondering why you should upgrade to Windows 10. Windows has a history of creating problems for users with every new release, especially with

Windows 8. We won't say that Windows 10 has zero issues, but it is the most secure and stable version of Windows available today. Windows 10 also comes with certain new features such as Cortana and Microsoft Edge that enhance the user experience.

Another reason you should upgrade to Windows 10 is that it will continue to receive support from Microsoft for a longer period in comparison to Windows 7 or Windows 8. However, before you start with the upgrade process, make sure that you backup your data.

Chapter Three: Useful Hacks for Windows 10

This chapter will teach you hacks for Windows 10, such as taking screenshots, disabling background applications, and saving battery.

There are numerous tips, tricks, and hacks you can employ to make your Windows 10 system faster and smoother.

Let us go through these tips and tricks one by one.

Minimizing all other windows except the one you need

There will be times when you have opened multiple windows and you want only one single window open that is the one you are working on. You can quickly minimize all the other windows and just keep the one you need open.

You can do this by clicking the title bar of the required window and dragging the window back and forth quickly, basically shaking it. After a few shakes, the other windows will automatically be minimized, and you will have just the one you need open.

Opening the secret Start Menu

You already know that the start menu can be launched by either clicking on the start button on your desktop or by hitting the Windows key on your keyboard. But there is also a secret start menu in Windows 10 through which you can conveniently access the important features such as command prompt, task manager, and control panel. There are two ways to access the secret start menu. The first method is by pressing the Windows + X key on your keyboard together. The other method is to right-click on the start button on your desktop.

Creating a Calendar Event without opening the calendar app

The latest update rolled out by Microsoft for Windows 10 lets you create events in your calendar directly from the taskbar. You don't even need to open the calendar app. You can do it by following the steps below.

1. Click on the time section that shows up on the extreme right-hand side of your taskbar.

2. Select the date where you wish to add the event.

3. Enter the details for the event such as name, location, and time. If you have created multiple calendars, click on the

down arrow and choose all the calendars on which you want this event to show.

4. Click on Save. The event will now show up on all your calendars across all your Microsoft devices.

Taking a screenshot

There are at least 8 ways to take a screenshot in Windows 10. If you need to screenshot your entire screen, you can simply press the Windows + Print Screen key on your keyboard, and that will save the picture to the Pictures > Screenshot folder.

If you want to screenshot a particular section of your screen, you can press the Windows + Shift + S keys on your keyboard. This will launch a tool called Snip & Sketch. The tool lets you drag and select a section of your screen and then snip it. The snipped section gets copied to your clipboard and you can paste it anywhere as required.

Using keyboard shortcuts to open Taskbar items

You may have pinned certain applications to your taskbar for easy access so that you can click on them and open them.

However, there are keyboard shortcuts you can use to open them and avoid clicking on the icons.

The keyboard shortcut is Windows + Number Key, where the number key would be 1 for the first icon, 2 for the second icon, and so on.

This comes handy if you are typing aggressively and do not want to lift your fingers from the keyboard to open an application. It would just be simpler in this instance to reach the Windows key and a number key.

Checking disk usage of apps

It is natural for a computer to start running slower when the disk space is shrinking. An easy way to increase disk space is by deleting apps that take a lot of space, especially the ones you do not use regularly.

You can check the disk usage for an app by going to:

Settings > System > Storage

Select the partition or the drive that you want to check the disk usage for, and then click on Apps & Games. This will list all the apps on your Windows 10 system and specify their disk usage. From there, you will be able to see which unused or unwanted apps are using disk space, and delete them.

Getting rid of Start menu ads

If you are running Windows 10 on its default settings, you will notice certain apps on the Start Menu that are not even installed on your system. These apps are called suggestions by Microsoft, but in reality, they are just ads for the apps in the Windows Store.

You can get rid of these ads by going to:

Settings > Personalization > Start

You will see an option there that reads Show suggestions occasionally in Start. Toggle this option off, and that will disable the ads on the start menu.

Shutting down background apps

Background apps are apps that collect information, send notifications, and keep themselves updated even when a user is not actively using them. This is useful but can end up leeching your data and battery.

You can easily control which apps run in the background and save some battery life and data. To do so, go to:

Settings > Privacy > Background apps

If you want to disable all apps from running in the background, you can simply disable the option for Let apps run in the background. If you want to disable individual apps from running in the background, you can toggle the button to off for individual apps from the list.

Use background scrolling

Windows 10 has a feature that lets you scroll up and down on all windows, irrespective of the window that is currently active. This feature is useful when you have multiple windows open and do not want to go through a particular window to scroll through it. For example, if there is a new window in which you wish to open the sub-menu options, this feature will help save you time as you will not need to alternate between two windows.

Let us try this out. Launch two applications on your Windows 10 system now, say any Internet browser and the notepad. Arrange both windows in a manner such that some part of each window is visible to you. Now, while you are working on one window, take your mouse pointer to the other window, and scroll. You should be able to scroll on that window, even if you are not active on it.

This feature is enabled by default in Windows 10. If it is not enabled, you can go to:

Settings > Devices > Mouse

From there, you can enable the option for Scroll inactive windows when I hover over them. After this is done, you will be allowed to hover on another window and still scroll without needing to be active on that window.

Show file extensions for files in File Explorer

The file extensions are hidden by default in the file explorer. This can be a problem for people who need to look at file extensions. For example, graphic designers need to know whether a file is JPG, PNG, etc.

To see the file extensions in the file explorer, you can follow the steps given below.

1. In the search option on your taskbar, search for File Explorer Options and click on it.

2. Click on the View tab in the window that pops up.

3. You will see a checkbox that says Hide extensions for known file types. Uncheck it and click on Apply.

You should now be able to see all the file extensions in the file explorer. The file explorer options utility also helps you to see hidden files or folders, empty drives, and more.

Use Focus Assist to remove distractions

It can be difficult to work on your Windows 10 system when notifications are popping up at regular intervals. The April 2018 update of Windows 10 added a feature called Focus Assist that helps you cut down on the notifications you receive.

You can set it up by going to:

Settings > System > Focus Assist

The tool has three options:

- **Off**: Keeping the focus assist off will ensure you get all the notifications from your Windows 10 system.

- **Priority**: This option lets you create a priority list of notifications that you wish to receive.

- **Alarms**: this option will ensure that you only get notifications for alarms, and all other notifications will be hidden.

You also get the option to switch Focus Assist on when you need, by defining a time window. For example, this could be set for when you are working or playing a game, where you do not want any distractions.

Link Microsoft OneDrive for cloud synchronization

Everyone loves free cloud storage. One of the best things about Windows 10 is that when you have linked your numerous Microsoft devices using the same Microsoft account, all your devices are synced to OneDrive. This means that your settings are retained across your devices. You will see the same wallpaper and lock screen background across all your Microsoft devices. This is not just for wallpapers. You will also be able to access the same email accounts across all your devices without the need to set it up multiple times. You can enable this feature while installing Windows by going to:

Settings > Accounts

Another advantage of OneDrive is you can store your files and pictures on the cloud, and they will be accessible across all your Microsoft devices.

Share Files

You are probably used to sharing files with your family members. The default method used for this is Email. However, with Windows 10, you can set up a network to share files with everyone in your house.

Click on the Start Button > Settings > Network & Internet > HomeGroup > Create HomeGroup

From here you can create a group of users that you want on your HomeGroup, and then, select files and folders that you wish to share with them.

Finding missing/corrupted files

There is a utility known as cmd. It stands for the command prompt and is very useful. One of the times you can use this utility is when you need to find files that your operating system needs to function properly. The utility can also help you fix file-related problems.

In the taskbar search field, type cmd. You will see the application for the command prompt. Right-click on it and select Run as administrator.

Now, to find missing files or corrupted files on your system, you can simply type the command:

sfc /scannow

If you want to check for problems on your hard disk, you can type the command:

chkdsk /f

Print PDF

The PDF format is compatible across platforms and operating systems. You can easily convert a text-based document into a PDF in Windows 10.

You can do this by opening the document in a text editor and giving the print command as you normally would. When you get the option to select the printer, instead of selecting an actual printer, you just need to select "Microsoft Print to PDF". This will just convert your document into a PDF and ask you for a location to save the PDF. You can then share this PDF with anyone you want using any online medium.

Recording screen activity

Now, with Windows 10, you can record your screen to watch a live gaming stream or a live video later.

This is very simple. When you are playing a video game online or watching a live video, simply click on the Windows + G keys on your keyboard. You will get a whole set of options through which you can record your entire screen.

Speeding up the start-up process for your system

There are a lot of processes that launch themselves by default when you start your computer. Some of these programs may be useful, while others may not be needed at all. The number of processes that launch at startup impact the speed of your computer. If you feel that your computer is starting to get slow during startup, you can cut down the number of startup processes from your task manager.

Right-click on the taskbar and launch the task manager. Select the Startup tab, and it will display all the processes and applications that launch at startup. You will see that some of them, or most of them, are enabled by default. You can sort through them and decide which ones are not needed and disable those. You can disable any process that has a medium or high impact on your system startup as long as they are processes you do not use.

Once you disable the unnecessary processes, you will see a significant improvement in your system startup time.

The task manager also shows all ongoing processes in your system, and you can kill an unwanted process that may be using a lot of unnecessary resources. To do so, right-click on the process and select End Task.

Adding your Xbox account

Not everyone owns the Microsoft Xbox but for those who do, Windows 10 makes it easy to link your Xbox account to your system through which you can manage your gaming activities. Another advantage of this feature is that you can stream your Xbox games directly to your Windows 10 desktop or laptop over a Wi-Fi connection. You can also purchase games for your Xbox using your Windows 10 system, and the games will be downloaded to your Xbox.

Chapter Four: Social Apps in Windows 10

In this chapter, we will discuss the important social apps in Windows 10, namely Mail, People, and Calendar. We will take you through the process of adding accounts, setting up an email account, sending and receiving photos, and more. You will also learn how to manage your contacts and your calendar.

Windows helps you to be social through the apps, Mail, People, and Calendar. You may have used these apps in the previous versions of Windows, but they come with a lot of new changes in Windows 10.

These three apps work beautifully together, keeping your contacts in one place.

Adding Accounts

When you open any of the three apps, Mail, People, or Contacts, for the first time on Windows 10, you are prompted to add not just Microsoft accounts, but accounts from other domains like Google or Yahoo. Adding all your account details in one place may sound scary to some, but it is completely safe. The information from your accounts is shared only if you approve it. If you do approve it, Windows will connect to your other accounts, such as Google and Yahoo, and import your contact details and other details to consolidate them in a single place.

Approving this is a good thing and saves a lot of time because all your accounts will be linked, and Windows will automatically log you into each of them, which can be very convenient.

You can follow the steps below to add your accounts to your Windows 10 system.

1. Click the start button and open the Mail app from the Start menu.

2. Add your accounts to the Mail app.

When you launch the Mail app for the first time, you will be prompted to add the most common email accounts such as Microsoft, Google, Yahoo, etc. If you created a Microsoft account for your login to Windows 10 during the installation, the email account for that account will show up in the Mail app already.

You can add other accounts by clicking on the Add Account button. You will then see the following list of accounts that can be added:

- Exchange: This is a business account for users that have Office 365 programs.

- Google: This is your Gmail account.

- iCloud: This is an apple account.

- Other Account: This is if you have a POP or IMAP email account with any other provider.

- Advanced Setup: This lets you add a web-based Email account or Exchange ActiveSync account.

To add a Google account, select the option for Google. The mail app will redirect you to a Google login website where you can enter your Google username and password and authorize Windows to access this account.

Similarly, you can add more accounts from the Mail app by clicking on Settings and selecting Accounts from the dropdown.

Repeat these steps every time you want to add a new account.

After you have added an account, the mail app will fetch all your emails from that account automatically. It will then use the information to fill the People app with the contacts, and the Calendar app with and calendar entries from your account.

The Mail App

Unlike the previous versions of Windows, Windows 10 comes with an inbuilt app to manage your mails. In comparison to the mail app on Windows 8, the Windows 10 mail app has support for POP and IMAP accounts. This means that you can configure an email account that you have purchased with even the smallest of providers, if you don't have an account with Google, Yahoo, etc.

Let us go through the interface of the Mail app in Windows 10.

You can launch the Mail app from the Start menu by clicking on the tile. The primary screen of your mail app will show you all the accounts that you have added on the first column of the mail app. You can click on any account to view the emails of that particular account.

Under the current email account that you are viewing, you will find the following mail folders:

Inbox

This folder is shown by default when you launch the mail app. It has all the emails you have received, with the latest emails at the top of the list. The mail app automatically checks for new emails in your account at regular intervals. However, if you do not want to wait, you can simply click on the sync button to see if any new emails have arrived. The sync button is two arrows making a circle next to your account's name. Once you click the button, it will immediately download new emails that have arrived on the email server.

Sent Items

This folder will list all the emails that you have sent to someone.

Drafts

There are times when you compose an email but are not ready to send it yet or just want to proofread it again later sometime before sending it. These emails will sit in Drafts. You can review them from there and send them whenever the time is right.

More

If you have created custom folders for sorting and categorizing your emails, these folders will appear under More. You can click on any folder, and the contents of that folder will appear on the right.

Composing and sending emails in the mail app

If you are ready to send a new email, you can follow the steps below to compose a new email and send it to a recipient's email address.

1. Launch the Mail app; choose the desired email account that you have already added, and then click on the plus

sign next to the account name. This will launch a blank space where you can start typing.

2. Type the recipient's email address in the To field. When you start typing the To address, the mail app will start scanning your contacts to see if the email address already exists there. It will show a dropdown of email addresses that may potentially match with the one that you are typing. If you see the email address, just click on it and the mail app will add it to the To field.

3. The subject line. This is where you can type the subject for your email. The subject line is optional, but it is advisable to always add a subject as many servers treat an email without a subject line as spam.

4. The body of the email. This is the huge blank space where you can write the content of your email. The mail app has a grammar and vocabulary check in place to correct any basic mistakes automatically.

5. Formatting, Insert, and Options. You will see a menu bar above the compose space for your email, which has three tabs as follows.

   a. Format: This option lets you format the text for the content in your email. You can change the font type, size, color, etc.

b. Insert: You can use this option to add attachments to your email. You can insert files, pictures, tables, and hyperlinks to your email through this option.

c. Options: Here, you can perform a final spellcheck on your email after you are done composing it.

6. Send the Email. You can finally click on the Send button on the top-right corner to send the email. The email is routed through the Internet to the recipient's mailbox. The speed at which the mail is sent and received depends on a lot of factors, but it will typically be received by the recipient within a couple of minutes.

If you do not want to send the email that you have composed, you can either save it to drafts or delete it permanently.

Reading a received mail

When you are connected to the Internet and receive a new email, the Mail app tile will automatically animate to show that a new email has arrived. To read the newly arrived email, follow the steps given below.

1. Launch the Mail app. In the mail app, select the email account that you need, and then click on the inbox folder.

2. Select the subject of the email that you wish to read. Click on the subject line of a newly arrived email or any other email that you wish to read.

3. After this, the mail app gives you several options to either do nothing, or take specific actions on the email that you just read:

    a. Nothing: Do nothing and just read the email and close the mail app after you are done.

    b. Reply: If you click on the Reply button, a new window will appear so that you can type a message as a response to the email. This window is similar to the Compose New Email window, with the exception that it already has the To address, and the subject filled. The original message will also appear at the bottom of your reply.

    c. Reply All: If there was more than one recipient marked on the original email that you received; the reply-all button will ensure that your response also goes to everyone in the To field.

    d. Forward: You can use this button to forward the email you received to someone new altogether who was not a part of the To field in the original email.

e. Delete: This button will delete the email and move it to the deleted items or trash folder of your email account.

f. Set Flag: This option will add a flag to the email so that it is highlighted in the inbox in case you wish to remember that it is an important email.

g. More: This option will give you a dropdown of a few more options. One of the useful options is Move, which allows you to move an email from one folder to another.

The People App

When you add an email address to the Mail app, Windows will fetch all the contacts on that email account and add it to the People app. This means that your people app will be automatically stocked up with a lot of contacts. The people app in Windows 10 is different compared to the one in Windows 8. It is not a social hub anymore and is more of an address book.

The people app manages itself automatically most of the time by adding contacts that you exchange emails with. However, you can also add contacts to it manually using the steps given below.

Adding contacts

1. Launch the People app. Open the People app from the People app tile in the start menu.

2. Click on the add contact button. If prompted, select the account to which you want to add the new contact.

3. If you have added more than one account to your Mail app, the People app will ask you where you want to add the new contact. You can add it to a particular account or select all accounts.

4. Fill the contact form. You will be presented with a contact form wherein you can add the name, phone number, email address, and other details for the new contact you are creating.

5. Click on the Save icon to save the new contact.

The Calendar App

When you add an email account to the Mail app, the calendars from those accounts are also automatically synced with the Calendar app in Windows 10. So, when you launch the calendar app for the first time, you may find that it is already stocked up with entries.

You can launch the calendar app by clicking on the calendar tile in the start menu. When you launch the calendar app for the first time, it will ask you to add accounts. However, if you have already added accounts though the mail app, the calendar entries will be populated automatically.

The calendar will show appointments or events that are associated with the accounts that you have added. You can change the view of the calendar by clicking on the Day, Week, Month, buttons on the top. Irrespective of the view of the calendar, you can navigate through the appointments or events by using the arrow keys in the corner of the screen.

Adding an Appointment

You can follow these steps to add a new appointment or event to your calendar.

1. Launch the Calendar app. You can click on the Calendar app tile on the start menu to launch it. If you are already working in the Mail app, you will also find a calendar icon within the Mail app from where you can launch the Calendar app.

2. Click on the New Event button. Doing so will launch a new blank template. You can add a name for the event here, the time, and the people that you wish to invite to the event.

3. Fill in the details. If you have entered more than one email account in your Mail app, you will need to decide which account the new Calendar event gets added to. You can again decide and choose one or more accounts to which the new Calendar entry will be associated.

4. Click on Save and Close. After you have created the event and added it to the respective calendar, you can click on save and then close the Calendar app.

You can edit or delete an event from the calendar as well. Simply open the Calendar app and select the required event. To delete the entry, simply click on the Delete button. If you want to edit an event, click on the entry on the calendar, make the required changes, then click on save and close the calendar again.

Chapter Five: Windows 10 Multimedia

In this chapter, we will teach you how you can use your Windows 10 system to share pictures with your friends and family. You will also learn how to copy pictures from your camera to your computer, how to use your Windows 10 laptop to watch movies, and how to organize a digital album for pictures imported from your digital camera.

Music

The Windows 10 music app is minimalistic and sticks to the essentials. It enables you to play music from your local computer or OneDrive through a few clicks. It also has an option where you can pay for a monthly pass for Microsoft Groove music that lets you play radio stations available on the Internet.

This is all that the Windows 10 music app lets you do. Unfortunately, it does not let you copy any music from a CD to your computer. Similarly, you cannot burn music from your computer onto a CD through this app. If you still have a computer with a CD drive, the app unfortunately does not support playing music from the CD drive directly.

If you have a desktop, you may also want to use the media player from the older versions of Windows: The Windows Media Player.

There is not a big difference between the Windows Media player in Windows 10 and the one from the older version except for one key feature; it does not play DVDs anymore.

In this section, we will discuss when you should alternate between the music app and the windows media player as per your requirements. This section will also tell you when you should ditch both these default apps and download a third-party app to suit your music needs.

The Music App

Keeping with the technologies today, the music app recognizes music only from your local drive, a USB drive, or the OneDrive. The music app does not support media such as CDs and DVDs.

However, if you want to purchase digital music, the Music app facilitates this well. When you launch the app for the first time, you will be able to see music that is stored on a local disk, or the OneDrive.

You can follow the steps given below to launch the music app and start listening to music.

1. Click the Music app tile that is available by default on the start menu.
   If you do not see the Music app tile on the start menu, you can click on the All Apps button and choose the

Music app from the alphabetical list that pops up. This will launch the Music app and present you with tiles of albums, artists, and songs. If you are opening the Music app for the first time, you will also have some welcome screens that you can choose to read through or skip.

2. Click on a tile to play the song. Click on a tile based on the album, artist, or song you want to hear, and the Music app will start playing the song based on your selection.

3. Adjust the music. You will see a bar from where you can control the music while it is playing. It offers options such as Previous, Shuffle, Repeat, Next, and Play/Pause.

You can adjust the volume by clicking on the little speaker icon on the bottom corner of the app bar. You can also control the master music from the desktop by clicking on the speaker icon on your taskbar.

The music app will continue to play music, even if you are working on other apps. You will need to return to the music app if you want to make any changes to the music that is currently playing.

Windows Media Player

Windows 10 still features the Windows Media Player that has been a staple for Microsoft operating systems for more than a decade. You can completely skip the Windows 10 Music app and still use the Windows Media Player to play your music. Locating the Windows Media Player in Windows 10 can be a task, as it is hidden in the start menu.

Let us go through the steps to locate and launch the Windows Media Player in Windows 10.

1. Click on the start button. When the start menu pops up, click on All Apps. This will show you all the apps in an alphabetically ordered list.

2. Scroll down to the entry for Windows Accessories. When the sub-entries show up for Windows Accessories, you will see the tile for Windows Media Player. Right-click on it and pin it to the Start menu for easy access in the future. You can also choose to pin it to the taskbar.

3. Return to the main start menu. Click on the Settings app.

4. Set Windows Media Player as the default app. In the Settings app, go to System and then go to Default apps. In the music player section, you will see the Music app listed as the default app. Click on it and from the dropdown, select Windows Media Player instead. This will now make

Windows Media Player the default app for music instead of the Music app.

5. Once you have completed this process, every time you double-click on a music file on your system, it will automatically open up in the Windows Media Player. You can also launch the Windows Media Player from the taskbar or the start menu where you pinned it earlier.

This does not mean that you have permanently uninstalled the Music app. You will just need to launch it from the start menu if you want to use it. When the app launches, you will still see all the music tiles in it.

Photos and Videos

Today, many people own a digital camera, and it is therefore important that Windows 10 supports digital cameras. You can simply plug your camera into your computer through a USB port and Windows will recognize it automatically. You can view your photos with a few clicks, and you will be able to copy the photos and videos from your camera to your computer.

Windows 10 also supports smartphones, and you can plug your smartphone in through a USB, and Windows will recognize it. You can then transfer photos and videos from your smartphone to your computer, too.

In this section, we will learn how to move your photos and videos from your camera or smartphone to your Windows 10 system.

Moving photos from your camera to your computer

Most cameras today have software that helps you move the photos from the camera to your computer. But it is not necessary to install this software and try to figure it out. Windows 10 has built-in support to fetch photos from almost every camera model, and smartphones, too. It also lets you create folders for photos related to a particular event.

The steps we are about to mention will work for all digital cameras and android smartphones. However, iPhone owners will need to use iTunes to copy their photos to their computer.

Follow the steps given below to import photos from your camera or smartphone to your computer:

Plug the camera or the smartphone to the computer via USB

You would have received a USB cable for your camera or smartphone when you bought it. For smartphones, this is usually the charging cable that you can unplug from the charging adapter and plug it into the USB port of your computer.

Switch the smartphone or camera on

Switch on your camera or smartphone and wait for Windows to recognize it. Launch the file explorer to view all the drives of your computer. If Windows has successfully recognized your smartphone or camera, it will list a new drive for it. Other times, it may just show your device as an icon in file explorer.

If you have connected your android smartphone, you may need to select what to do from the settings of your android phone. You can select whether you just want it to charge or if you want to use it for media transfer.

Transfer the photos and videos

Once you see the icon for your camera in the file explorer, right-click on it and select Import Pictures and Videos. You will see two options after this:

1. Review, Organize, and Group Items to Import

This is when you have pictures in the camera or smartphone from various events and want to group them accordingly. It will automatically create a new folder for every event and copy the photos to them. The process takes time, but it saves you the trouble of manually organizing your photos, especially when they are in the hundreds or thousands.

2. Import All New Items Now

This option is useful when your smartphone or camera has photos from a single event. It simply copies all the photos in a single folder.

Note: There is a link for More Options that lets you change the location where Windows copies your photos. It will also give you the option to keep or delete the photos from the camera after the copying is completed.

Import all new Items Now

You will see a box for tags where you can add a short description, for example, Summer Break. Click Next. Windows will then copy all your photos to a folder named Summer Break. All the photos that are copied will also have the prefix Summer Break. After the photos are copied, simply head to the Pictures folder and click on the folder name to view all the copied photos. Adding a description for the photos also helps you locate them easily in the future. You can simply search for the description in the start menu search option and Windows will list the photos for you.

Review, Organize, and Group Items to Import

Windows checks the timestamp of all the photos in your smartphone or camera to organize it into groups.

Adjust the Grouping

You will see a pop up that shows the groups created by Windows. If you do not like the grouping created by Windows, you can use the slider at the bottom that says Adjust grouping. If you want the time interval for the groups to be shorter for the timestamps of your photos, slide to the left. For example, you can sort groups by every half an hour that the photos were taken. You can keep sliding to the right to increase this time interval. If you take the slider to the extreme right, it will put all photos into a single folder.

Approve the groups, the folder names, and description tags

You can give a customized name and description to every group if needed. You can also add tags to make it easy to find the photos later. Once you have done this, click on the Import button to import all the photos.

Windows will start copying the photos from the camera or smartphone to your computer. While the copying is in progress, the progress popup will show you a checkbox that says, "Erase after importing". You can check this box to delete the photos from your camera or smartphone automatically after they are copied to the computer.

Viewing Photos

There are two ways to view photos in Windows 10: The photo app and the photo viewer. The photo viewer has been a staple utility on Windows operating systems for over a decade.

Photos App

Microsoft, however, wants you to adopt the Windows 10 Photos app. It sorts your photos in two ways.

1. Collection

When you open the Windows 10 Photos app in the collection view, you will see all the photos on your system in the order that they were taken. It does not leave anything out, which can make it a bit hectic to go through all of them and delete the unwanted ones.

2. Albums

In this view, the Windows 10 Photos app will group the photos and name them according to the day that they were taken. It even removes the duplicates automatically.

In both these modes, when you open a photo in the full-screen mode, you're presented with the following options:

Return to collection

This will take you back to the thumbnail view for your photo collection. It is a leftwards arrow on the top left corner of the Photos app.

Share the Photo

Clicking this button will give you a list of apps through which you can share the photo. If you already have an email configured in Windows 10, you can use the email app to share your photo, too.

Slide Show

When you click on this button, the screen will get cleared and the app will start showing you all the photos one by one like a slide show. It shows every photo for approximately five seconds and moves to the next photo. You can simply click on any photo to stop the slide show.

Enhance

This option adds a retouch to your original photo to enhance it and make it look better. If you think the original looked better, you can click on enhance a second time to disable the effects added by enhance.

Edit

Clicking this button will give you a menu to edit the photo. You can edit the photo as per your needs, and then click on the X button to exit the edit mode.

Rotate

As the name suggests, this button rotates the picture by 90 degrees every time you click it.

Delete

If you come across a blurred photo or a photo you don't like, you can use this button to delete it.

More Menu

This button will drop a menu that has some additional options through which you can copy or print a photo. You can also set the photo as your computer's lock screen and see other details of the photo such as name, resolution, size, and timestamp.

Zoom

Click on this button and then use the buttons on the bottom right to zoom in or zoom out of the photo.

You can exit the Photos app by clicking on the X symbol in the top right corner of the window.

Windows Photo Viewer

The photos app in Windows 10 is a good option to view photos, but some people still prefer the good old Windows Photo Viewer that has been a part of Windows since 1997. This is again hidden in Windows 10 and is not listed on the start menu.

Follow the steps given below to view photos using the Windows photo viewer.

1. Click on the start button to launch the start menu, and then click on the file explorer link. This will launch the file explorer.

2. In the file explorer, click on This PC, and it should list down all the different locations on your computer. Select Pictures. This will open the pictures folder where all your photos are usually stored.

3. Open the folder of the photos you wish to view in the Pictures folder. Right-click on any of the photos and hover over Open With. You will get a list of applications to open the photo with. Select Windows Photo Viewer.

This will open the selected photo in the Windows Photo Viewer. You can now simply use the left and right arrow keys on your keyboard to navigate through the remaining photos in the same folder.

Keeping your photos organized

It will always be tempting to create a new folder for photos in the pictures directory and dump all your photos there. However, this system is messy when you want to find a particular photo a few days later. The import tools in Windows 10 do a good job of importing and organizing your photos into folders as per timestamps and tags. There are a couple of other tips that will help you organize your photos better:

- Assign the four most common tags to your photos that are Home, Travel, Holidays, and Relatives. These tags will make it easy to locate photos that are taken at home, while traveling, while on a holiday, or of relatives, later on when you need to find a photo.

- The tag provided by you is assigned to every batch of photos that are imported. After the common tag is assigned, spend some time to assign some custom tags to photos manually after the import is completed. You can assign multiple tags to a photo by separating tags with a semicolon. This will also help you easily locate photos in the future.

Chapter Six: Upgrading to Windows 10 for Free

We have already mentioned previously that the free upgrade to Windows 10 officially ended in June 2016. At the time of writing however, there are some Windows enthusiasts who report that you can still upgrade to Windows 10 for free if you have a Windows system running Windows 7 or Windows 8.1. This can be done using Microsoft's free upgrade tools, and you do not need a product key. After installation, you also get a digital license that states that your copy of Windows 10 is activated and you're good to go.

We would assume that no one told the people who run the activation servers for Microsoft that the offer has ended. It is true and verified by most users that the free upgrade to Windows 10 is still working without any issues. This upgrade is more important today than it was before, as Microsoft has now officially ended support for Windows 7.

Note that this upgrade will get you the Windows 10 Home version and you can upgrade to Windows 10 Pro if you have a product key for one of the previous Windows versions of 7, 8, or 8.1 Pro or Ultimate.

In this chapter, we will cover the basics of installing Windows 10 as an upgrade. We will also discuss the various licensing issues you may encounter.

Upgrading an old system to Windows 10

If you have a system running on a genuine copy of Windows 7 with Home, Pro, or Ultimate versions, or Windows 8/8.1 with Home or Business versions, that have been activated properly, you can follow this guide to upgrade your system to Windows 10.

There are a few preliminary checks you should complete before you can begin:

- Check that your current version of Windows is properly activated. This is a very important check if you have reinstalled Windows after the initial install.

- Check for recent updates for network and storage drivers.

- Check if your BIOS have received any latest updates. If yes, update your BIOS to the latest version available. This is very important if you have a system that you purchased before 2015, which is before the launch of Windows 10.

- Backup all your data to an external hard disk or a cloud. You can do a full backup for your Windows 7 system to an external hard drive using the inbuilt backup option. This option is also available for Windows 8 and Windows 10.

Just search for the string sdclt.exe in your search box and hit enter. This will launch the backup option. Choose the Create a System Image option.

- If you have any third-party software for security such as a firewall or an antivirus, disable it to ensure that it doesn't interfere with the upgrade. You can always reinstall that software after completing the upgrade.

- Finally, disconnect unwanted external devices like USB drives and hard drives.

With the above checks passed, the next step is to download the Windows 10 Upgrade tool. You can download it from the Microsoft website, or by using the link below:

https://www.microsoft.com/en-us/software-download/windows10

Click on the Download Tool button. After the file gets downloaded, launch the executable file that will launch the Media Creation Tool.

It should show you a screen that asks if you would like to either:

- Upgrade this PC now

- Create installation media for another PC

If you have downloaded this tool on the machine you want to upgrade, and if you want to upgrade only one machine, you can select the Upgrade this PC now option. This will upgrade your system to the latest version of Windows 10. Depending on your hardware and Internet speed, the upgrade process will typically take around an hour.

If you want to upgrade more than one machine to Windows 10 or just don't want to risk a direct upgrade encountering a failure, you can select the second option. This will save the Windows 10 installation files to an ISO image or a USB drive. After the download completes, you can run the Windows 10 setup manually on any Windows 7 or Windows 8 system. Unfortunately, this will not work on a Windows XP or a Windows Vista system.

The next steps will depend on which download option you select.

USB Flash Drive

Insert the flash drive to which you downloaded the Windows 10 installation file into a USB slot on the system where you wish to install Windows 10. Launch the file explorer, navigate to the USB drive, and then click on Setup to launch the Windows 10 installer. Do note that this is not a bootable USB and you cannot boot into it to upgrade your system to Windows 10. You must run the setup after logging into your existing licensed copy of Windows 7 or Windows 8.

ISO file

If you have saved the Windows 10 installation as an ISO image, you need to mount the ISO to launch the installer. In a system that has Windows 8, you can simply double-click on the ISO file to launch it in a virtual drive. If you have a Windows 7 system, you will need a third-party application to mount the ISO. You can download WinCDEmu from https://github.com/sysprogs/WinCDEmu/releases for this purpose. Double click on Setup to start the installation.

Once the installer begins, you can just follow the instructions provided by the Windows 10 installer to complete the upgrade process. You will not be asked for a product key at any point during the upgrade process. And after the upgrade completes, your copy of Windows 10 will be a digitally licensed copy of the latest Windows 10 version. You can verify this by going to:

Settings > Update and Security > Activation

You should see a message that says, "Windows is activated with a digital license,".

Moreover, all your data and apps will be retained.

The digital license is now embedded onto your device. This means that you can now perform a clean install of Windows 10 on the same device in the future if the need arises. This will mostly be needed if you are upgrading your hard disk to an SSD and you want to reinstall Windows 10 again. You can do this without worrying, as the digital license will be linked automatically again to the new installation. You will not need a product key, and Windows 10 will get activated automatically when you connect to the Internet.

Conclusion

Windows 10 is the most stable operating system to be launched by Microsoft. It is the perfect operating system for both home and business users. Windows 10 has been built keeping in mind the legacy versions of Windows such as Windows 98, XP, Vista, 7 as well as Windows 8.

Microsoft has taken into consideration the requirements of the older generation as well as the newer generation while designing and developing Windows 10.

You should now feel prepared to begin using Windows 10 and customizing it to suit your own personal preferences. I hope you have enjoyed this book and have found it to be helpful!

www.ingramcontent.com/pod-product-compliance
Lightning Source LLC
Chambersburg PA
CBHW070854070326
40690CB00009B/1834